First World War
and Army of Occupation
War Diary
France, Belgium and Germany

4 CAVALRY DIVISION
Divisional Troops
Royal Army Service Corps
Auxiliary Horse Transport Company (577 Company A.S.C.)
1 January 1917 - 31 May 1917

WO95/1158/10

The Naval & Military Press Ltd
www.nmarchive.com
Published in association with The National Archives

Published by

The Naval & Military Press Ltd

Unit 10 Ridgewood Industrial Park,

Uckfield, East Sussex,

TN22 5QE England

Tel: +44 (0) 1825 749494

www.naval-military-press.com

www.nmarchive.com

This diary has been reprinted in facsimile from the original. Any imperfections are inevitably reproduced and the quality may fall short of modern type and cartographic standards.

© **Crown Copyright**
Images reproduced by permission of The National Archives, London, England, 2015.

Contents

Document type	Place/Title	Date From	Date To
Heading	WO95/1158/10		
Heading	Bde 4 Cav Div Troops Aux (H) Transport Coy (577 Coy Asc) 1917 Jan-1918 Mar From 1st Indian Cav Div Box 1172 To GHQ Troops Box 144		
Heading	War Diary of No. 577 Auxiliary Horse Transport Company, A.S.C., 4th Cavalry Division. From 1st January 1917 To 31st January 1917		
War Diary	Friville	01/01/1917	31/01/1917
Heading	War Diary. of Capt. E.H. Moseley. O.C. 577 Auxiliary Horse Transport Coy. A.S.C. 4th Cavalry Division. From 1st To 28th February. 1917 Volume		
War Diary	Friville	01/02/1917	28/02/1917
Heading	War Diary of Captain E.H. Moseley. O.C. 577 Auxiliary Horse Transport Coy. A.S.C. 4th Cavalry Division. From 1st to 31st March 1917 Volume.		
War Diary	Friville	01/03/1917	18/03/1917
War Diary	Field	19/03/1917	22/03/1917
War Diary	Albert	23/03/1917	31/03/1917
War Diary	Friville	01/03/1917	18/03/1917
War Diary	Field	19/03/1917	22/03/1917
War Diary	Albert	23/03/1917	31/03/1917
Heading	War Diary. of Captain E.H. Moseley. 577 Auxiliary Horse Transport Coy. A.S.C. 4th Cavalry Division From 1st April 1917 To 30th April 1917 Volume.		
War Diary	Aveuloy	01/04/1917	03/04/1917
War Diary	Irles	04/04/1917	12/04/1917
War Diary	Aveuloy	13/04/1917	13/04/1917
War Diary	Vauchelles	14/04/1917	24/04/1917
War Diary	Authievel	25/04/1917	27/04/1917
War Diary	Doullens	28/04/1917	30/04/1917
War Diary	Aveuloy	01/04/1917	03/04/1917
War Diary	Irles	04/04/1917	12/04/1917
War Diary	Avuloy.	13/04/1917	13/04/1917
War Diary	Vauchelles	14/04/1917	24/04/1917
War Diary	Authievel	25/04/1917	27/04/1917
War Diary	Doullens	28/04/1917	30/04/1917
Heading	War Diary of Captain E.H. Moseley. O.C No 577 Auxiliary Horse Transport Coy. A.S.C. 4th Cavalry Division. From 1st May To 30th June 1917 Volume		
War Diary	Doullens	01/05/1917	13/05/1917
War Diary	Aveuloy	14/05/1917	15/05/1917
War Diary	Fries	16/05/1917	16/05/1917
War Diary		17/05/1917	17/05/1917
War Diary	Mons en Chausse	18/05/1917	31/05/1917
War Diary	Doullens	01/05/1917	13/05/1917
War Diary	Aveuloy	14/05/1917	15/05/1917
War Diary	Fries	16/05/1917	16/05/1917
War Diary		17/05/1917	17/05/1917
War Diary	Mons en Chausse	18/05/1917	31/05/1917

Heading	War Diary of Captain E.H. Moseley O.C. 577 Auxiliary Horse Transport Company Army Service Corps. 4th Cavalry Division From 1st June to 30th 1917 Volume		
War Diary		01/06/1917	09/06/1917
War Diary	Mons en Chaussee	09/06/1917	30/06/1917
Heading	War Diary of Captain E.H. Moseley. O.C. 577 Auxiliary Horse Transport Coy. A.S.C. 4th Cavalry Division From 1st July To 31st 1917 Volume		
War Diary		01/07/1917	07/07/1917
War Diary	Mons. en Chaussee	08/07/1917	31/07/1917
Heading	War Diary of Captain E.H. Moseley. O.C. 577 Auxiliary H Transport Coy A.S.C. 4th Cavalry Division From 1st to 31st August 1917 Volume.		
War Diary		01/08/1917	10/08/1917
War Diary	Mons en Chaussee	10/08/1917	31/08/1917
Heading	War Diary of Captain E.H. Moseley O.C 577 Auxiliary & Transport Coy A.S.C 4th Cavalry Division From 1st to 30th September 1917 Volume		
War Diary		01/09/1917	04/09/1917
War Diary	Mons en Chaussee	05/09/1917	30/09/1917
Heading	War Diary of Captain E.H. Moseley Commanding 577 Auxiliary Horse Transport Coy. Army Service Corps 4th Cavalry Division From 1st To 31st October 1917 Volume		
War Diary		01/10/1917	01/10/1917
War Diary	Mons en Chaussee	02/10/1917	31/10/1917
Heading	War Diary of Captain E.H. Moseley. O.C, 577 Auxiliary Horse Transport Coy. Army Service Corps. 4th Cavalry Division From 1st to 30th November 1917 Volume.		
War Diary		01/11/1917	06/11/1917
War Diary	Mons. en Chaussee	07/11/1917	20/11/1917
War Diary	Athies	21/11/1917	22/11/1917
War Diary		23/11/1917	23/11/1917
War Diary	Mons en Chaussee	24/11/1917	25/11/1917
War Diary	Mons	26/11/1917	30/11/1917
Heading	War Diary of O.C. 577 Coy A.H.T. 4th Cav. Divn. Dec. 1st to 31st 1917		
War Diary		01/12/1917	03/12/1917
War Diary	Mons en Chaussee	04/12/1917	31/12/1917
War Diary	Mons-En-Chaussee	01/01/1918	03/02/1918
War Diary	Harbonniers.	04/02/1918	04/02/1918
War Diary	Vers	05/02/1918	27/02/1918
War Diary	Harbonieres	28/02/1918	28/02/1918
War Diary	Villers-Carbonnel	15/03/1918	23/03/1918
War Diary	Between Villers Carbonnel and Estrees	24/03/1918	31/03/1918
War Diary	Friville	01/03/1917	18/03/1917
War Diary	Friville To St Roquier	19/03/1917	19/03/1917
War Diary	St Roquier To Carnaples	20/03/1917	20/03/1917
War Diary	Carnaples To Talmas	21/03/1917	21/03/1917
War Diary	Talmas To Albert	22/03/1917	22/03/1917
War Diary	Albert	23/03/1917	31/03/1917
War Diary	Aveuloy	01/04/1917	04/04/1917
War Diary	Irles	05/04/1917	12/04/1917
War Diary	Avuloy	13/04/1917	13/04/1917
War Diary	Vauchelles	14/04/1917	25/04/1917

War Diary	Authieule	26/04/1917	27/04/1917
War Diary	Doullens	28/04/1917	13/05/1917
War Diary	Aveuloy	14/05/1917	15/05/1917
War Diary	Fries	16/05/1917	16/05/1917
War Diary		17/05/1917	17/05/1917
War Diary	Mons en Chausse	18/05/1917	31/05/1917

WO 95/11581 9/8/10

BEF

4 CAV DIV TROOPS

AUX (H) TRANSPORT COY
(577 COY ASC)

1917 JAN — 1918 MAR

FROM 1st INDIAN CAV DIV Box 1172

TO GHQ TROOPS Box 131 144
           also 144

SERIAL NO. 31/2.

Confidential
War Diary
of

No. 577 AUXILIARY HORSE TRANSPORT COMPNAY, A.S.C., 4TH CAVALRY DIVISION.

FROM 1st JANUARY 1971 TO 31st JANUARY 1917. 1916.

Army Form C. 2118.

WAR DIARY
or
INTELLIGENCE SUMMARY.
(Erase heading not required.)

Instructions regarding War Diaries and Intelligence Summaries are contained in F. S. Regs., Part II. and the Staff Manual respectively. Title pages will be prepared in manuscript.

Place	Date	Hour	Summary of Events and Information	Remarks and references to Appendices
FRIVILLE	1917 Jan 1 2 3 4 5 6 7 8 9 10 11 12 13 14 15 16 17 18 19 20 21 22 23 24 25 26 27 28 29 30 31		Routine &c.	

J. Hopkins Lt.
for
OC 149th Co & A.O.Div.

Serial No 313.

CONFIDENTIAL

WAR DIARY.
OF
CAPT. E.H. MOSELEY. O.C.
577 AUXILIARY HORSE TRANSPORT COY.
A.S.C.
4th CAVALRY DIVISION.

FROM 1st TO 28th FEBRUARY, 1917.

VOLUME

Army Form C. 2118.

WAR DIARY
or
INTELLIGENCE SUMMARY
(Erase heading not required.)

Instructions regarding War Diaries and Intelligence Summaries are contained in F. S. Regs., Part II. and the Staff Manual respectively. Title Pages will be prepared in manuscript.

Place	Date	Hour	Summary of Events and Information	Remarks and references to Appendices
Friville	Feb 1/17			
"	2			
"	3			
"	4			
"	5			
"	6			
"	7			
"	8			
"	9			
"	10			
"	11			
"	12		No change. Duties as usual. E.O.M.	
"	13			
"	14			
"	15			
"	16			
"	17			
"	18			
"	19			
"	20			
"	21			
"	22			
"	23			
"	24		O.Teows left with Lucknow Brigade. E.M.	
"	25		No change. Duties as usual. E.M.	
"	26		" " " " " "	
"	27			
"	28			

Army Form C. 2118.

WAR DIARY
or
INTELLIGENCE SUMMARY

(Erase heading not required.)

Instructions regarding War Diaries and Intelligence Summaries are contained in F. S. Regs., Part II. and the Staff Manual respectively. Title Pages will be prepared in manuscript.

Place	Date	Hour	Summary of Events and Information	Remarks and references to Appendices
Fripille	Feb 1st			
	2			
	3			
	4			
	5			
	6			
	7			
	8			
	9			
	10			
	11		No change. Routine as usual.	
	12			
	13			
	14			
	15			
	16			
	17			
	18			
	19			
	20			
	21			
	22			
	23			
	24			
	25			
	26			
	27			
	28			

Serial No. 313

CONFIDENTIAL

WAR DIARY.
OF
Captain E.H. Moseley, O.C.
577 Auxiliary Horse Transport Coy.
A.S.C
4th Cavalry Division.

From 1st to 31st March 1917

VOLUME.

577 AUX. H.T. COY A.S.C.
31 MAR. 1917
4TH CAVALRY DIVISION

WAR DIARY or INTELLIGENCE SUMMARY

Army Form C. 2118.

Place	Date MARCH 1917	Hour	Summary of Events and Information	Remarks and references to Appendices
FRIVILLE	1st TO 18		Duties as usual. No change 6 P.M.	
FIELD	19		Marched to Ft. RIQUIER with Reserve Rations for 3 days. Billeted for the night. 2 P.M.	
"	20		Marched to CARNAPLES Billeted for night. 2 P.M.	
"	21		Marched to THALMAS Billeted for night. 2 P.M.	
"	22		Marched to ALBERT. CAMPED. 4 P.M.	
ALBERT	23		Ordinary duties. Handed over remainder of Reserve Rations to O.C. T.S.O. 1 P.M.	
"	24		Ordinary duties 9 P.M.	
"	25		Ordinary duties 9 P.M.	
"	26		Ordinary duties 9 P.M.	
"	27		10 Teams for duty with SALKOFF Bg.A 2 P.M.	
"	28		19 Teams for duty at BAPAUME. 2/Lieut J.L. AUSTIN 8 P.M.	
"	29		Duties as usual 9 P.M.	
"	30		Duties as usual 9 P.M.	
"	31		Duties as usual 2/Lieut J.L. AUSTIN reached for duty with Guards Bg.A R.F.A. 2 P.M.	

C.W. Maclellan Capt.
O.C. 577 Aux. H.T. Coy A.S.C.
47th Barnsley Division

Army Form C. 2118.

WAR DIARY
or
INTELLIGENCE SUMMARY
(Erase heading not required.)

Instructions regarding War Diaries and Intelligence Summaries are contained in F. S. Regs., Part II. and the Staff Manual respectively. Title Pages will be prepared in manuscript.

Place	Date	Hour	Summary of Events and Information	Remarks and references to Appendices
	MARCH 1917			
FRIVILLE	1st to 18		Duties as usual. No change. E.H.M.	
FIELD	19		Marched to Jt ROQUIER with Reserve Rations for 3 days. Billeted for the night. E.H.M.	
"	20		Marched to CARNAPLES Billeted for night. E.H.M.	
"	21		Marched to THILMAS Billeted for night. E.H.M.	
"	22		Marched to ALBERT. CAMPED. E.H.M.	
ALBERT	23		Ordinary duties. Handed over remainder of Reserve Rations to O.S.S.O. E.H.M.	
"	24		Ordinary duties. E.H.M.	
"	25		Ordinary duties. E.H.M.	
"	26		Ordinary duties. E.H.M.	
"	27		10 Teams for duty with SAILKOTE Bde. E.H.M.	
"	28		19 Teams for duty at BAPAUME. 2/Lieut J.L.AUSTIN E.H.M.	
"	29		Duties as usual. E.H.M.	
"	30		Duties as usual. E.H.M.	
"	31		Duties as usual. 2/Lieut J.L.AUSTIN recalled for duty with Guards Bde R.F.A. E.H.M.	

E.H.Morley Capt.
O.C. 5TH Aust H.T.Coy A.S.C.
His Cavalry Division

Confidential

WAR DIARY.

OF

CAPTAIN E.H. MOSELEY.

577 AUXILIARY HORSE TRANSPORT COY.

A.S.C.

4th CAVALRY DIVISION

FROM 1st APRIL 1917.

TO 30th APRIL 1917.

VOLUME.

Serial No. 3/3

WAR DIARY or INTELLIGENCE SUMMARY

Army Form C. 2118.

Place	Date	Hour	Summary of Events and Information	Remarks and references to Appendices
AVULUY	APRIL 1		No Change. Usual duties. 2/Lieut G. Amelin left to report on probation to R.F.A. GUARDS Bde. F/C. G. Thulow reported for duty vice 2/Lt G. Amelin.	
	2		C.S.M. Mayes reported detachment at BAPUME shelled N°3 43+5 4am 6&7 Bombr M. Shafer, Shoesmith Shuck & horse killed. E/R.M.	
	3		No change. Usual duties. E/R.M.	
IRLES	4		Marched IRLES. Camp Map 57C. G.26.3. Very bad full of shell holes. E/R.M.	
"	5 to 12		No Change. Duties as usual. E/R.M.	
AVULUY	13		Marched AVULUY. Camped 57C.W.16.3. E/R.M.	
VAUCHELLES	14		Marched to VAUCHELLES. Camped 57C.I.33". E/R.M.	
	15 to 24		2/Lieut G.C. Thulow left to report to G.R.F.C. on probation. No change. duties as usual. E/R.M.	
AUTHIEVEL	25		Marched AUTHIEVEL 11.45 p.m. Camped 57 F.B.26 and from outskirt Chaudry. E/R.M	
"	26 & 27		No change 6pm.	
DOULLENS	28		Marched to DOULLENS. 11.30 a.m. Camped 5/10 in Citidal Moat. E/R.M.	
"	29 & 30		No change. Usual duties. E/R.M.	

Army Form C. 2118.

WAR DIARY
INTELLIGENCE SUMMARY
(Erase heading not required.)

Instructions regarding War Diaries and Intelligence Summaries are contained in F.S. Regs., Part II. and the Staff Manual respectively. Title Pages will be prepared in manuscript.

Place	Date	Hour	Summary of Events and Information	Remarks and references to Appendices
AVELUY	APRIL 1		No Change. Usual duties. 2/Lieut E. Lavalin left to report on probation to R.F.A. Guards Bde. 2/Lt E. E. Thurston reported for duty vide 2/Lt Lavalin.	
	2		G.3.M. Mileage reported detachment at BAPAUME shelled. N° 34345 Gnr 6ᵖ. Blanchflr shrapnel shock 1 horse killed. E.P.M.	
	3		No change. Usual duties E.P.M.	
IRLES	4		Marched IRLES. Camp Map 57.C. Q.26.2. Very bad full of shell holes. E.P.M.	
"	5 to 12ᵗʰ		No Change. Duties as usual. E.P.M.	
AVELUY	13		Marched AVELUY. Camped 57.C. W.16.2. E.P.M.	
VAUCHELLES	14		Marched to VAUCHELLES Camped 57.C. I.33.9. E.P.M.	
	15 to 24ᵗʰ		2/Lieut E.C. Thurston left to report to G.R.F.C. on probation. No change. duties as usual. E.P.M.	
AUTHIEUVEL	25		Marched AUTHIEUVEL 11.45 p.m. Camped 57.D. B. 26 or d. Good water and standings. E.P.M.	
"	26 to 27ᵗʰ		No change. E.P.M.	
DOULLENS	28		Marched to DOULLENS. 11.30 a.m. Camped in Citidal Moat. E.P.M.	
"	29-30		No change. Usual duties. E.P.M.	

Serial No. 313.

Confidential.
War Diary
of
CAPTAIN E. H. MOSELEY. O.C.

N° 577 AUXILIARY HORSE TRANSPORT COY.

A.S.C.

4th CAVALRY DIVISION.

FROM 1st MAY TO ~~31st MAY 1917~~ 30th June 1917.

VOLUME

577 AUX. H.T. COY A.S.C.
31 MAY. 1917
4TH CAVALRY DIVISION

Army Form C. 2118.

WAR DIARY
or
INTELLIGENCE SUMMARY.
(Erase heading not required.)

Instructions regarding War Diaries and Intelligence Summaries are contained in F. S. Regs., Part II. and the Staff Manual respectively. Title pages will be prepared in manuscript.

57 AUX. H.T. COY.A.
31 MAY 1917
4TH CAVALRY DIV.

Place	Date	Hour	Summary of Events and Information	Remarks and references to Appendices
DOULLENS	MAY 12 to 8th		No change - usual duties. E/M	
"	9th		Lieut J.A. Haymen joined Coy for duty from Base Depot étaves E/M	
"	10 to 13th		No change - usual duties. E/M	
AVELUOY	14th		Marched to AVELUOY. Camped. Map Ref. 57D. W.16.8. E/M	
"	15		No change - usual duties E/M	
FRIES	16		Marched to FRIES. Camped Map Ref. 62B. G.24. E.&E/M	
MONS en CHAUSSÉ	17th		Marched to MONS en CHAUSSÉ, camped Map Ref. 62B. P.25.d. E/M	
"	18 to 23		No change - usual duties - E/M	
"	24		Lieut J.A. Haymen reported sick - removed to convalescent Depot. E/M.	
"	25 to 31		No change usual duties. E/M	

Army Form C. 2118.

WAR DIARY
or
INTELLIGENCE SUMMARY
(Erase heading not required.)

Instructions regarding War Diaries and Intelligence Summaries are contained in F. S. Regs., Part II. and the Staff Manual respectively. Title Pages will be prepared in manuscript.

Stamp: 677 AUX. H.T. COY A.S.C. 31 MAY 1917 — 4TH CAVALRY DIV

Place	Date	Hour	Summary of Events and Information	Remarks and references to Appendices
DOULLENS	MAY 1st to 8th		No change - usual duties E/H.M.	
"	9th		Lieut. J.A. Hayman joined Coy for duty from Base Depôt Havre E/H.M	
"	10 to 13th		No change - usual duties E/H.M.	
AVELUY	14th		Marched to AVELUY. Camped. Map Ref. 57D, W.16.d. E/H.M	
"	15		No change - usual duties E/H.M	
FRIES	16		Marched to FRIES. Camped Map Ref. 62B, G.24 E/H.M.	
MONS en CHAUSSEE	17th		Marched to MONS en CHAUSSEE, camped Map Ref. 62B P.26 d E/H.M	
CHAUSSE	18 to 22		No change - usual duties E/H.M.	
"	24		Lieut J.A. Hayman reported sick - removed to Convalescent Depôt E/H.M	
"	25 to 31st		No change usual duties E/H.M	

"Confidential"
War Diary
of

Captain E.H. Moseley. O.C.
577 Auxiliary Horse
Transport Company
Army Service Corps.
4th Cavalry Division

From 1st June to 30th 1917

Volume

E.H. Moseley Capt.

Army Form C. 2118.

WAR DIARY
or
INTELLIGENCE SUMMARY.
(Erase heading not required.)

Instructions regarding War Diaries and Intelligence Summaries are contained in F. S. Regs., Part II. and the Staff Manual respectively. Title pages will be prepared in manuscript.

Place	Date	Hour	Summary of Events and Information	Remarks and references to Appendices
MONS en CHAUSSEE	JUNE 1st to 9th		Usual Company duties Farm. No change – nothing to report.	
	10th		Ten Teams with 109 G. Wagons employed on Agricultural work Farm.	
	11-13		Usual Company duties Extraordinary	
	14th		14 Pairs Agricultural Work Farm.	
	15th		Usual Coy duties S.P.M.	
	16th		Usual Coy duties. Lieut. L. Bruce Major from Brewers Farm reported Sr. unit went by Staff.	
	17-19		Usual Coy duties. Sergt 55 Remain'd Medical form to CHAPPELLET STA. to Cap. B&C Bn Blain Div'n.	
	20th		Lieut L. Bruce Major to Canne through of Coy. Authority G.M.F. G.H.Q. NºA.S. 16047.	
	21-25		Usual Coy ordinary Lieut. L. O'Brien Major to Canne through of Hamilton S. unit	
	26-30		Usual Coy duties Extraord.	
	*		Returned the 10th and 30th inst. 750 animals have been furnished daily for Farm and Agricultural work. The average being 47 daily in addition to ordinary station form.	

B.A. Moseley Capt.
O.C. 577 Supplying troops through Cav Coy
4th Cavalry Division

Serial No. 313.

CONFIDENTIAL

WAR DIARY
OF
CAPTAIN E. H. MOSELEY. O.C.

577 AUXILIARY HORSE TRANSPORT COY.

A.S.C.

4TH CAVALRY DIVISION

FROM 1ST JULY TO 31ST 1917.

VOLUME

Army Form C. 2118.

WAR DIARY
or
INTELLIGENCE SUMMARY.
(Erase heading not required.)

Instructions regarding War Diaries and Intelligence Summaries are contained in F.S. Regs., Part II. and the Staff Manual respectively. Title pages will be prepared in manuscript.

Place	Date JULY	Hour	Summary of Events and Information	Remarks and references to Appendices
MONS-env-	1st to 7th		Usual Convoying Duties and FARMS WORK. E.M.M.	
CHAUSSEE	8th		Usual Convoying Duties and FARMS. WORK. Lieut. A. Henderson temp.attached for duty from H.Q. A.S.C. 4th Cav.	
	9th		Usual Convoying Duties & FARMS. WORK. E.M.M.	
	10th		Usual Convoying Duties & FARMS. WORK. No. T3/126665 S/Sjt Adamson R. recalled to FARM WORK. E.M.M.	
	11-12		Usual Convoying Duties on FARMS WORK. E.M.M.	
	13th		Usual Convoying Duties. FARMS WORK. No. T3/016620 S/S Robinson M. Awarded 1st Cl. FARM WORK C.W.	
	14th		Usual Convoying Duties FARMS WORK. One G.S. Wagon Team + 2 Drs Transferred to Bde from 5 A.C. & B.W. 4. 1pm	
	15-18	4.12	2 Riding and 5 L.D. Remounts received from Base Depot. Usual Convoying & Farms Works. E.M.M.	
	19		L/c A Hyman evacuated to Saf aux Cl. struck off strength of Convoy 717/17. 3.15pm	
			Lieut A Henderson to Reserve Park for duty - 2/Lieut A.W.W. Riley from Reserve Park for duty.	
	20-31st		Usual Duties & Farms Works. E.M.M.	

E.H. Morony Captain
O.C. Aux (H) Transport Coy
4th Cavalry Division

4TH CAVALRY DIVL.
AUX. H.T. COMPANY.
(No. 577 COY. A.S.C.)
No. 31/1/17

Serial No. 313

Confidential

War Diary of

Captain E. H. Moseley.

O.C. 577 Auxiliary H. Transport Coy
A.S.C.

4th Cavalry Division

From 1st to 31st August

1917

VOLUME.

Army Form C. 2118.

WAR DIARY
or
INTELLIGENCE SUMMARY.
(*Erase heading not required.*)

Place	Date	Hour	Summary of Events and Information	Remarks and references to Appendices
MONS-en-CHAUSSEE	AUGUST 1917 1st to 10th		} Usual Routine & Coy Duties E.F.M.	
	11th to 20th		} Usual Routine & Coy Duties E.F.M.	
	21st to 30th		} Usual Routine & Coy Duties E.F.M.	
	31st		Usual Routine & Coy Duties E.F.M.	

R. Mowrey Capt. A.S.C.
O.C. A.P.O. Coy – 4th Cavalry Division

Confidential   Serial No: 313

WAR DIARY OF
Captain E. H. Moseley.
O.C. 577 Auxiliary H. Transport Coy.
A.S.C.
4th Cavalry Division
From 1st to 30th September.
1917
VOLUME

WAR DIARY or INTELLIGENCE SUMMARY.

Army Form C. 2118.

Place	Date	Hour	Summary of Events and Information	Remarks and references to Appendices
MONS en CHAUSSEE	SEPTEMBER 1st to 4th		Usual Duties. E.&M.	
	5		Usual ratio Returned off leave from United Kingdom. E.&M.	
	6 to 10th		Usual Duties E.&M	
	11th		Lt L Bruce Major, 15 R.Dragoons & personnel on detachment Left Salouges 25 mp POZIERS E.M.	
			C.S.M Mayo.C. Seniors fell from his horse. Sept. Usual duties	
	12		C.S.M. Mayo.C. admitted to hospital. Invalided E.M.	
	13 to 17		Usual duties. Two Owels Bar Registration E&M.	
	18 to 20		Usual duties E&M	
	21st		Usual duties. Visited detachment on Salouges Strip POZIERS. all is well E&M.	
	22 to 24		Usual duties. E&M.	
	25		2nd Lieut J. McN. Kelly. 15 R.S. Dragoons rejoined to POZIERS. Relief Lieut H. Power H/fre. S&M	
	26		Usual duties E&M	
	27		Lieut L. Bruce Major returned to H.Q. Relieved by 2nd Lt. H. McKelvy. all personnel E&M.	
	28		Usual duties. 1 R.Dragoon to ADIX LE CHATEAU 19 Dragoons to FRIXECOURT. St Lt 63rd Divisions. S.M.	
	29		Usual duties 1 G.S. Dragoon to TOUTENCOURT. duty with 63rd Dragoons E.M.	
	30		Usual duties. E.M., Day 2 Fuel & Forage S&M.	

E.H. McNally Capt.
A.S.C. A.T. Coy
4th Cavalry Division

Confidential
WAR DIARY OF
Captain E. H. Moseley
Commanding 577 Auxiliary Horse Transport Coy,
Army Service Corps
4th Cavalry Division
From 1st to 31st October
1917
VOLUME

313

577 AUX. H.T. COY A.S.C.
31 OCT. 1917
4TH CAVALRY DIVISION

WAR DIARY or INTELLIGENCE SUMMARY

Army Form C. 2118.

Place	Date	Hour	Summary of Events and Information	Remarks and references to Appendices
MONS EN CHAUSSÉE	OCTOBER 1st		2/Lieut. J. McN. KELLEY to relieve detachment. Reserve Park at MONTAUBAN from POZIÈRES. E.A.M.	
	2nd		S/S/t. BURGOYNE Returned from Convoy to TOURNECOURT with M.G.S. Wagons. E.A.M.	
	3		S/S/t. Burgoyne with 5 wagons from MONTAUBAN Dump- nothing received. 1 G.S. wagon from ADX. I. LE CHATEAU and one G.P. Wagon from FINXECOURT. Convoy with Mrs. Wagons E.A.M.	
	4th		Three Nag. Parks in by. Stoboyed E.A.M.	
	5th to 9		Usual duties. no change E.A.M.	
	10th		Detachment of 10 G.S. Wagons leave Montauban under 2/Lt. McNHelley — relieved by R.L. Bruce Major. E.A.M.	
	11,12,13		Usual duties — no change E.A.M.	
	19		Lieut. L. Bruce Major to MONTAUBAN to inspect detachment and take out winter clothing for men. E.A.M.	
	20th		Lieut. L. Bruce Major returned from MONTAUBAN. reported all in order. E.A.M.	
	21 — 23		Usual duties. no change E.A.M.	
	24th		Detachment at MONTAUBAN relieved by Lieut. L. Bruce Major. E.A.M.	
	25 — 28		Usual duties. No change E.A.M.	
	29th		No. 403678 & Kn. Smith. A.E. tried by F.G.C.M. for absence without leave from Remounts W.K.V. E.A.M.	
	30		No Change. Usual duties. E.A.M.	
	31		No Change. Usual duties. E.A.M.	

E.M. Moseley Capt.
vd. A.M.T.Coy.
4th Cavalry Division

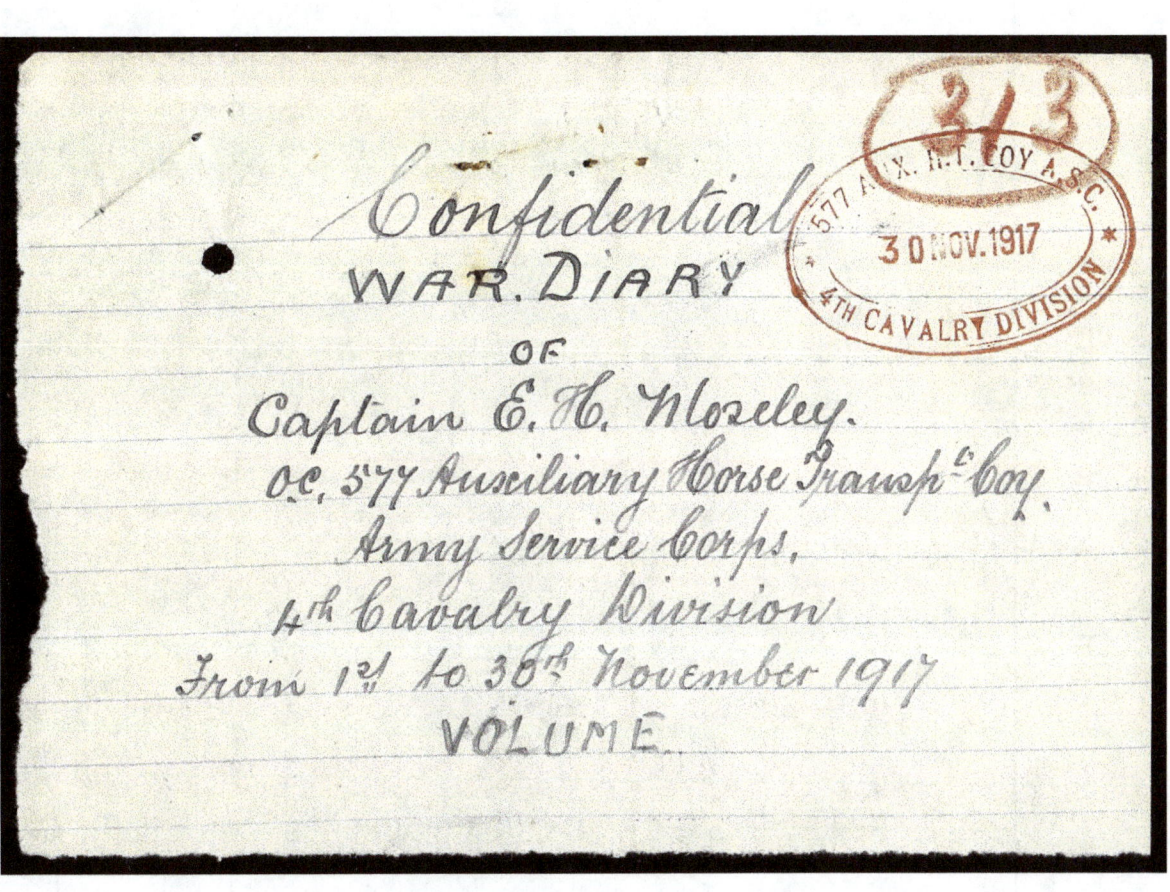

Confidential
WAR DIARY
OF
Captain E. H. Moseley.
O.C. 577 Auxiliary Horse Transp. Coy.
Army Service Corps.
4th Cavalry Division
From 1st to 30th November 1917
VOLUME

Army Form C. 2118.

WAR DIARY
or
INTELLIGENCE SUMMARY.
(Erase heading not required.)

Instructions regarding War Diaries and Intelligence Summaries are contained in F. S. Regs., Part II. and the Staff Manual respectively. Title pages will be prepared in manuscript.

Place	Date	Hour	Summary of Events and Information	Remarks and references to Appendices
MONS on CHAUSSEE	NOVEMBER 1917 1st	6th	Usual duties no change. E/M.	
	7th		2/Lt M. Kelly relieved Detachment at MONTAUBAN under 2/Lt. Bruce Major E/M.	
"	8 to 11		Usual duties no change E/M.	
"	12th		Orders to be ready to load up Ammunition. E/M.	
"	13th		4 G.S. Wagons "Jeures" to Ammunition Dump, QUINCONCE, PERONNE, loaded up G.S.W. with 270 Cases H.E. 1080 rounds, 14 G.S.W. Shrapnel 1620 rounds = 2700 rounds 13 Feb. 18 G.S.W. with 648000 rounds S.A.A. & 10 cases of FLARES — Lieut L. Bruce MAJOR (attached) to 4th RESERVE PARK for duty — Detachment on duty MONTAUBAN, returned to H.Q. E/M.	
"	14 to 17th		Usual duties - no change. E/M.	
"	18th		Loaded 1 days safe Rations per man also 20 lbs oats per animal. Issued 1 days fb Rations to each man, also Leather Jerkins. Inspected Gas Helmets E/M.	
"	19, 20		Usual duties - horses up early to march at 4 hours notice E/M.	
ATHIES	21st		Marched ATHIES 8.15. a.m. Reported arrival to Major Lance O/C "B" ECHELON.	
"	22nd		Stand to awaiting Orders E/M.	
MONS en	23		Returned to MONS. E/M.	
CHAUSSEE	24 to 25th		Stand to. awaiting further Orders. E/M.	

Army Form C. 2118.

WAR DIARY
or
INTELLIGENCE SUMMARY.
(Erase heading not required.)

Instructions regarding War Diaries and Intelligence Summaries are contained in F. S. Regs., Part II. and the Staff Manual respectively. Title pages will be prepared in manuscript.

Place	Date	Hour	Summary of Events and Information	Remarks and references to Appendices
MONS	NOVEMBER 1917 26th to 28		Stood to waiting orders EdM.	
"	29		Returned 2700 rounds 13 br - 648000 rounds S.A.A. and 1250 Flares to Ammunition Dump QUINCONCE, PERONNE. EdM.	
"	30		Usual duties - no change EdM.	

E.H. Morley Capt.
O.C. No.57 Aux. Coy
4th Cavalry Division

[Stamp: 57 AUX. H.T. COY A.S.C. 30 NOV. 1917 4TH CAVALRY DIVISION]

Confidential

War Diary
of
O.C. 577 Coy A.H.T.
4th Cav. Divn.

Dec. 1st to 31st 1917

Army Form C. 2118.
313

WAR DIARY
or
INTELLIGENCE SUMMARY.
(Erase heading not required.)

Confidential

Place	Date	Hour	Summary of Events and Information	Remarks and references to Appendices
Mons en Chaussée	1/10	3ᵈ	Standing to awaiting orders 8KM.	
	4ᵗʰ to 8ᵗʰ		Usual duties no change 8KM	
	9 - 10		Thunderstorms in operation 8KM;	
	11 - 12		Usual duties no change. 4.A.L.W. Kelly sick to TINCOURT.2ᵈ J.M.E.R. Tim.Hy. wounded	Tim.Hy. wounded
	13 14		Usual duties. No change. J.M.E.R.	
	15 16		Usual duties 2 horses evacuated under orders of Vety Sp. on 16— J.M.E.R.	
	17 18		Usual duties. No change. J.M.E.R.	
	19		Usual duties No change. J.M.E.R.	
	20		Usual duties Sergt. J.N. WAUGH A.S.C. assumed command. J.M.E.R.	
	21		Usual duties Ditto	
x	22ⁿᵈ 23ʳᵈ 24ᵗʰ 25ᵗʰ		Usual duties Ditto	
	26 27		" On 27.19. Capt. J.N. WAUGH A.S.C. to Tempy Command 4ᵗʰ Res. Park. To C.O.R. 2ⁿᵈ Lieut. J.M. N. KELLY A.S.C. to Tempy command 597 coy. P.P. To C.O.R.	
	28		Usual duties — 25 G.S. wagons brought in from LE MESNIL as work completed there. J.M.E.R.	
	29		" 13 G.S. Wagons to Pail head — Drawing rations. 1 horse died. 9.a.m. under vety orders. J.M.E.R.	
	30		" Do Do — A.C.S. Eastes with 21⁴ 2ⁿᵈ T.C. J.M.E.R.	
	31		" Do Do. 2.A.S. wagons to M.T. B.a.M. N. Carrière J.M.E.R.	
			Do 31/12/19 - J.M. Kelly 2ⁿᵈ Lt. A.S.C. Comdg 597 coy A.H. Gd. Cav Div	

31.12.19

No. 544 Auxy. Transport Coy; A.S.C.
att. 1st Cavalry Division

WAR DIARY
of
INTELLIGENCE SUMMARY
(Erase heading not required.)

January, 1916.

Army Form C. 2118.

Place	Date	Hour	Summary of Events and Information	Remarks and references to Appendices
MONS-EN-CHAUSSEE	1st to 3rd/1/18.		Usual duties. No change.	J.M.R. Major
	3rd to 5th/1/18.		" " No change.	J.M.R. Major
	6th to 8th/1/18.		" " "	J.M.R. Major
	9/1/18. to 10/1/18.		" " "	J.M.R. Major
	11/1/18		No change. Gas scheme came into force from 5 P.M. 7th - bus was employed at midnight.	J.M.R. Major
	12/1/18		Gas scheme begun - Continued. 2/Lt. S.C.G.FIELDER. A.S.C. reported for duty. Began erecting shiv-go-gahs (?) with assistance and motor transportation	J.M.R. Major
	13/1/18		" continued - Continued erection of spincted wood protection	J.M.R. Major
	14/1/18		" discontinued. Reconnaissance made to new park now occupied by unit - EAST of line drawn N & S through V8 Central	J.M.R. Major
	15/1/18		Gas scheme began. 5 P.M. "Jesmel" to be used instead of pails. Roadhead duties ex	J.M.R. Major
	16/1/18 - 19/1/18		" " " " " other rail head duties. 10 G.S. Wagons on duties	J.M.R. Major
	18/1/18		duty to MONTIGNY FARM. 1 Horse Diad. 4 wounded mules divided Do	Do
	19/1/13.		13 G.S. Wagons to R. Head only. Do	Do
	20/1/18.		13 G.S. " + 10 G.S. Wagons + 12 G.L. Wagons to R. Head. Do	Do
	21/1/18		1 TANK WAGON to VERMAND. 5 G.S. Wagons on Road. 13 G.S. Wagons + 12 G.S. Wagons to R. Head.	J.M.R. Major
	22/1/18.		Gas scheme ceased from 6 P.M. 21/1/18. - 12 wagons to R. Head - 50 on road. Men of company who have not been inoculated - interviewed - I arranged protecting humid inoculated in afternoon	J.M.R. Major

Army Form C. 2118.

WAR DIARY

(Erase heading not required.)

Instructions regarding War Diaries and Intelligence Summaries are contained in F. S. Regs., Part II and the Staff Manual respectively. Title pages will be prepared in manuscript.

Place	Date	Hour	Summary of Events and Information	Remarks and references to Appendices
MONS- EN- CHAUSSEE	23.1.18.		2 G.S. wagons & limbers at VILLERS CARBONNEL - exchanged - (relieves) - Usual duties.	WK
	24.1.18.		Usual duties. BOX RESPIRATORS of unit inspected by A.N.C.O. of Gas officer's staff.	
	25.1.18.		Usual duties. ANIMALS of unit inspected by A.D.V.S. 4th Cav: Div.	
	26.1.18.		Part hrd duties discontinued - 5 wagons on road - 2 wagons regrined from VILLERS CARBONNEL.	
	27.1.18.		10 G.S. wagons of detachment at MONTIGNY FARM regined. 5 wagons on road. OATS ration which was 10 lbs to all animals.	
	28.1.18.		No duties excepting watering rations. 3 G.S. wagons to H.Q. 4th Res: Div. JODHPUR - SIRBAR	
	29.1.18.		1 Driver to ABBEVILLE for a course of shoeing.	
	30.1.18.		General harness & wagon cleaning. General harness wagon cleaning.	
	31.1.18.		Animals etc of unit inspected by O/C A.P.C. 4th Cav: Div.	

J McSherry
Capt. A.V.C.
Comnd. 599 Coy A.V.C. 4th Cav: Div.

WAR DIARY

Army Form C. 2118

577 Coy A.H.T.
4th Res. Div.

February 1915

Place	Date	Hour	Summary of Events and Information	Remarks and references to Appendices
MON-EN-	1.2.18.		Daily return of T.S.A. received from 5/02 Co ½ 02: 1 W. Off & 3 Drivers of 2nd Cav. Regt. Copy of report received at H.Q. 4/2 G.S. Wagons to Divn. 1 H.Q. 4/2 G.S. Wagons to Paris-Gadi. 14 M horn 4 H. Dial Ref. 1 G.S. Wagon on leave.	Jn Cork Jn Iffley
CHAUSSEE	2.2.18.		General harness cleaning — 14 Lindhorn (4 M horn) 4 INH C Vers G later on Inspection starting. Sent ambulance to 2 N.C.O.'s of Incoming Units	Joseph Iffley
	3.2.18.		" " " " — Handed over 2nd H.T. Co. W.O. of 2nd Cav. Regt. Copy attached	Iffley. Jn Cork
HARBONNIERS	4.2.18.		Marched from MONS-EN-CHAUSSEE to HARBONNIERS with 5/KATE BRIGADE – 5 G.S. WAGONS.	Iffley Jn Cork
			1 WATER CART – Billetted the night at HARBONNIERS.	
VERS	5.2.18.		Marched from HARBONNIERS to VERS. at about	
"	6.2.18.		Began drawing mil. rations from railhead – SALEUX	
"	7.2.16.			
"	8.2.15		CAPT. T. N. NAUGH from H.Q. Can Divi Res Park took over command of this Coy.	Iffley Pele
			4 G.S. wagon attached for the March. Regained rank, 1 G.S. wagon returning with Skeleton Burbon. Lt Kelly to U.K. on Leave	
"	9.2.15		Pt Whitaker transferred to Norfolks Regt. at his own request.	Pele
			" D. Jones " " 2nd A.W.B. " " "	
	10.2.18		7 G.S. Wagons 30 L.D. horses & 15 Mn's to 1 Nor. H.T. Depot ABBEVILLE & Struck off Strength Arslt. Can Corps O 348 A/5 2. 18	Pele Jn Cork
	11.2.15		Nothing to report	Pele Jn Cork

Army Form C. 2118.

WAR DIARY
or
INTELLIGENCE SUMMARY.

(Erase heading not required.)

5.77 Co. A. V.T. Cy
4th Can. Div

Place	Date	Hour	Summary of Events and Information	Remarks and references to Appendices
VERS	12.2.18		Dr Morgan transferred to 2nd Sup B at his own request	
"	13.2.18		Nothing to report	
"	14.2.18		One rider accidentally killed by bolting on a recent L.S. wagon & L.D horses & 2 drivers to CAYEUX	
	15.2.18		Nothing to report	
	16.2.18		" " "	
	17.2.18		A fire occurred in the village at 1.30 A.M. The fire was got under by the men of the Coy. No damage to Govt property.	
	18.2.18		Nothing to report	
	19.2.18		1 G.S. wagon & 2 horses & 2 drivers rejoined from CAYEUX	
	20.2.18		1 " " " " rejoined from Thooper Anchor	
	21.2.18		Nothing to report	
	22.2.18			
	23.2.18		Mark 10 G.S wagons were sent to Thooper Lancer & Thooper Car F Am. in exchange for 7 Centaur'd pattern.	
	24.2.18		Nothing	

J Wentworth Capt.

WAR DIARY
or
INTELLIGENCE SUMMARY. 4th Cav. Div.

577 Coy A.H.T.

Army Form C. 2118.

Place	Date	Hour	Summary of Events and Information	Remarks and references to Appendices
VERS	25.2.18		Nothing to report	
"	26.2.18			
"	27.2.18		Company marched from VERS enroute to join II Army	
HARBONIERES	26 2/75			

Scarborough Capt RE
O.C. 4th Can. Div. A.H.T.Coy

28/9/18

WAR DIARY A.H.T. COPY. A.H. Bn. Dist. 5th Army Corps.

Army Form C. 2118
3/3

March 1918.

INTELLIGENCE SUMMARY
(Erase heading not required.)

Place	Date	Hour	Summary of Events and Information	Remarks and references to Appendices
VILLERS-CARBONNEL	15.3.18		Usual road duties. 2 negroes in from 2 Middlesex for repair + 2 returned to unit.	
	16.3.18	"	"	
	19.3.18	"	Wagon cleaning etc. Visited MISERY. Road WK.	
	18.3.18	"	Interviewed D.A.D.T. at 5th Army.	
	19.3.18	"	" " at Corps H.Q. at ER. "Rue Longue" Bridge dug + work at La Chapelette.	
			Inspected my men at work.	
	20.3.18	"	Visited MARCHELPOT + distribument Bay.	
			Distributed pay at Villers Carbonnel + Marche-pot.	
	21.3.18	"	" " Marchelpot.	
	22.3.18	"	" " Foucaucourt.	
	23.3.18	"	Road Wagon? Trains in civvies moved. Marched from Villers Carbonnel to FOUCAUCOURT. From FOUCAUCOURT to CAPPY. Convoy was attacked by German aeroplane.	
Between Villers Carbonnel and Estrées			From FOUCAUCOURT to FAY. + from FAY to CAPPY. followed by shell fire. Lt DONE received 2 bullet wounds + 5 horses also were wounded by machine gun fire.	
	24.3.18.		Marched from CAPPY to FOUCAUCOURT. "Yin Lorri" Q orders waiting us with IV Bn. (Paid.) did so + found Major Chaplin S— in T.Off. Reports arrived of men Major R at Guillaucourt	
	25.3.18.		Marched from Guillaucourt to CAYEUX-EN-SANTERRE. back to GUILLAUCOURT from there to and up Kid Yd of Labour groups (comdg Off 15 Col. Steward) & marched through from Guillaucourt to BOVES. From BOVES to LE PARACLER where Austral Corps 2353 Wt W35/1454/6/009000 5k5. D. B&l LerA. Newspaper Wireless from LE PARACLER to VILLERS BRETTONNEUX	
	26.3.18.		MARCHED FROM VILLERS BRETTONNEUX to CACHY	

WAR DIARY

Army Form C. 2118.

Place	Date	Hour	Summary of Events and Information	Remarks and references to Appendices
	26/3/18		Marches from CACHY to BACUEL	[initials]
	27/3/18		" BACUEL to LONGPRE	[initials]
	28/3/18		" LONGPRE to MAYONNEVILLE	[initials]
	29/3/18		Starting to at MAYONNEVILLE, Bivouac Rd	[initials]
	30/3/18		" MEN & HORSES 2% in billets	[initials]
	31/3/18		Usual routine work. Stables - harness cleaning 9%	[initials]

MAYONNEVILLE
31.3.18.

J. [signature] Lt. A.S.C.
Comdg. A.M. Coys. 14th Bn: Inf.
5th Army Group.

Army Form C. 2118.

WAR DIARY
or
INTELLIGENCE SUMMARY.
(Erase heading not required.)

Place	Date	Hour	Summary of Events and Information	Remarks and references to Appendices
FRIVILLE	1st to 31st January 1917		Usual Routine daily. S.S.M.	

E.H.Moreley Capt.
a.a. A.v.s. H.Q. 6ot
4th Cavalry Division

Army Form C. 2118.

WAR DIARY
or
INTELLIGENCE SUMMARY.
(Erase heading not required.)

Instructions regarding War Diaries and Intelligence Summaries are contained in F. S. Regs., Part II. and the Staff Manual respectively. Title pages will be prepared in manuscript.

Place	Date	Hour	Summary of Events and Information	Remarks and references to Appendices
FREVILLE	1st FEBRUARY to 28th		Issued Routine daily to S.W.	

E.P. Mosley Capt.
O.C. Aux Horse Transp "Coy"
1st Cavalry Division

Army Form C. 2118.

WAR DIARY
or
INTELLIGENCE SUMMARY.
(Erase heading not required.)

Instructions regarding War Diaries and Intelligence Summaries are contained in F.S. Regs., Part II. and the Staff Manual respectively. Title pages will be prepared in manuscript.

Place	Date	Hour	Summary of Events and Information	Remarks and references to Appendices
	MARCH 1919			
FAVILLE	1st to 9th		Usual Routine – No change. E.A.M.	
"	10		2/Lieut J. Austin interviewed by G.S.O. R.A. asks him to be kind to R.F.A. E.A.M.	
"	11 to 14		Usual Routine - No change E.A.M.	
"	15th		2/Lieut J.L. Austin proceeded to St ROQUIER to arrange billets for party A.H.T. & Recce Partis returning from duty with LUCKNOW Bde. E.A.M.	
"	16		Usual Routine - 2/Lieut J Austin returned. Billets cancelled E.A.M.	
"	17		Usual Routine - Case of measles reported - Billet disinfected E.A.M.	
"	18		Usual Routine. No change	
FAVILLE to St ROQUIER	19		Formed a Reserve Park (19 G.S. Wagons v teams from Reserve Park) loaded at Divisional Dump WIDNCOURT with 300 Boxes Iron Rations (British) 6000 Iron Rations (Indian) 6000 Rations - 2 G.S. Wagons GUR - 55,500 lbs Oats - marched 10.30 a.m. via CHEPPY - ABBEVILLE to St ROQUIER. Weather very bad. arr. 10 p.m. Camped on road and marked square. One horse stranded E.A.M.	
St ROQUIER to CARNAPLES	20		Marched 10.30 a.m. via DERNUEL to CARNAPLES arr. 6 p.m. Billets E.A.M.	

Army Form C. 2118.

WAR DIARY
or
INTELLIGENCE SUMMARY.
(Erase heading not required.)

Instructions regarding War Diaries and Intelligence Summaries are contained in F. S. Regs., Part II. and the Staff Manual respectively. Title pages will be prepared in manuscript.

Place	Date	Hour	Summary of Events and Information	Remarks and references to Appendices
	MARCH. 1917			
CARNAPLES TO TALMAS	21st		Marched 3.30 p.m. roads in an awful condition. Weather very bad. Snow and rain — arr. Talmas 10.30 p.m. Bivouaqued on Road. E.T.M.	
TALMAS TO ALBERT	22		Marched 8.25 a.m. Via WARLOY–SENLIS. arr. ALBERT 9.30 p.m. Bivouaqued. Weather very bad. Snow & rain. Cold. E.T.M.	
ALBERT	23		Pitched camp and parked wagons at AVULOY. Arrival awaited standard E.T.M.	
"	24		Horses taken down Rations sent to S.S.O. 26 Teams wagons under Lieut Phillips to bring in forage left behind by other units. E.T.M.	
"	25		25 G.S. wagons & Teams to SIALKOTE Res to carry Iron trps. Lt. Phillips and 26 Teams returned. G.T.D. E.T.M.	
"	26		19 G.S. wagons & Teams returned to Reserve Park. Bow Regd's list Jat 10 A.M. E.T.M.	
"	27		Capt Waleigh. 10 F.T. Wagons & Teams SALKOTE LUCKNOW Bde B.T. O'Duty	
"	28		Lieut J. R. Austin & 10 G.S. wagons, Teams to BAPAUME for duty E.T.M.	
"	29		Moved Camp to 5.Y.C. W.16. 6. E.T.M.	
"	30		Issued Rations E.T.M.	
"	31		C.S.M. Khyn C Relieved 2nd Lieut J. Austin at BAPAUME who proceeds to QUARTRS Divisional ARTILLERY. On probation E.T.M.	

E. F. Moseley Capt.
O.C. Aux Horse Transp. Co.
4th Cavalry Division

WAR DIARY
or
INTELLIGENCE SUMMARY
(Erase heading not required.)

Army Form C. 2118.

Instructions regarding War Diaries and Intelligence Summaries are contained in F.S. Regs., Part II. and the Staff Manual respectively. Title Pages will be prepared in manuscript.

Place	Date APRIL	Hour	Summary of Events and Information	Remarks and references to Appendices
AVELUY	1st	—	2/Lieut. J. L. Anstin left Bay to report to R.F.A. Guards Brigade on one month's probation with a view to transfer if suitable. 2/Lieut E. E. Thulin reported for duty vice 2/Lt. G.L. Anstin. 2nd Lt G.J.M. Mayo to detachment at Bapaume reported being shelled. No 75, E343 Cpl Pm. Blanch, M. Storr - slight shell shock. One Horse killed. B.T.O. Sailkote Bde. reported 1 Horse dead. Observation 8 t/M	
"	2			
"	3		No change. Usual duties. 8 t/M	
	4		Marched to IRLES. Camp full of Shell holes. Very bad. Maps Go Map 57G 26 & E t/M	
IRLES	5		No change. Usual duties. Horses died exposure + exhaustion. Reported to O.E. A.R.P. Bad condition of animals and wagons returned from duty on detachment with SIALKOTE Bde 6 t/M	
	6		No change - 2 Horses died exposure and exhaustion. 8 t/M	
	7		No change - 2 Horses died exposure and exhaustion + evacuated, debilitated. 8 t/M	
	8		No change - 3 Horses destroyed by order of Vet Officer exhausted. 1 evacuated. Rec'd 11 Mules remounts. 8 t/M	
	9		No change - 1 Horse evacuated debilitated to M.H.O.W. Mobile Vet. Sec. 8 t/M	
	10		No change - 1 MULE died exposure + exhaustion. 8 t/M	
	11		No change - "Q" Batt. reported loss of one horse. Supplied another. Reported to A.D.V.S. bad state of ammunition. 8 t/M	
	12		No change - 1 Mule died exposure and exhaustion. 8 t/M	
AVULDY	13		Marched AVULDY. Camp 57°C W.16". 2 Horses died + 2 destroyed before leaving. exhaustion. 1 Mule evacuated. 8 t/M	
VAUCHELLES	14		Marched VAUCHELLES. Camp 57°C.I.33". One Horse died one Mule evacuated on march. 8 t/M	
"	15		No Change. 2/Lieut E. E. Thulin left Coy to report to C. R.F.C. for duty on probation 8 t/M	
	16-24		No Change - Usual Routine - Many men with bad feet through mud + wet 8 t/M	
	25		Marched 11.30 a.m. to AUTHIEUL Good Billets + Horse standings with plenty of water. 8 t/M	
AUTHIEUL	26-27		Usual Routine - No change. 8 t/M	
DOULLENS	28		Marched DOULLENS - Camped in MOAT of CITIDAL. MEN in Billets - both good. 8 t/M	
	29-30		Usual Duties - No change. 8 t/M	

R.H. Moseley. Capt.
O.C. Divl H.Q. Coy
4th Cavalry Division

WAR DIARY or INTELLIGENCE SUMMARY

Army Form C. 2118.

Place	Date MAY	Hour	Summary of Events and Information	Remarks and references to Appendices
DOULLENS	1st to 9th		Workshops - usual duties.	
"	10th	12.1	Usual duties. Lieut J.A. Heymann reported for duty from Base E/T.M.	
"	10 to 13th		Usual duties. E/T.M.	
AVELUY	14th		Marched to AVELUY. Camped MAP REF. 57D. W.16.C. E/T.M.	
"	15		Usual duties. E/T.M.	
FRIES	16		Marched to FRIES. Camped MAP REF. 62C. C.24.C. E/T.M.	
MONS en CHAUSSE	17		Marched to MONS en CHAUSSE. Camped MAP REF. 62C. P.26.d. E/T.M.	
CHAUSSE	18 to 23		Usual duties E/T.M.	
"	24		Lieut J.A. Heymann reported sick – To Convalescent Depot E/T.M.	
"	25 to 31		Usual duties. E/T.M.	

E.J. Markey Capt.
O.C. Aux. Horse Transp't Coy
4 Cavalry Division